CREATIVE MUSIC

Robert Pace

UP AND DOWN

1. "Shape" the melody pattern in the air as you sing the finger numbers.
   Notice this melody moves by *steps*.
2. Sing the finger numbers — clap the rhythm.
3. Play this on your arm as you move each finger and sing its number.
4. Now sing the numbers and play it on the piano keyboard.

ASSIGNED_____ COMPLETED_____							COMMENTS:
WEEK	M	T	W	Th	F	S	Su	
1st								
2nd								
3rd								

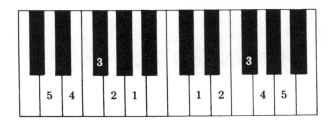

MELODY PATTERN
Left Hand

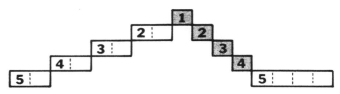

MELODY PATTERN
Right Hand

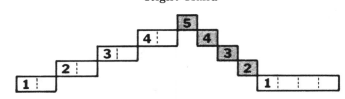

Here is another place to play "Up and Down."

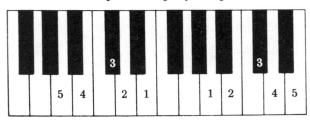

Left Hand

Teacher's Music

Right Hand

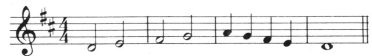

SKIPS

ASSIGNED___ COMPLETED___ COMMENTS:								
WEEK	M	T	W	Th	F	S	Su	_____
1st								_____
2nd								_____
3rd								_____

Again:

1. "Shape" the melody pattern in the air as you sing the finger numbers.

  2. Sing the finger numbers — clap the rhythm.

    3. Play this on your arm as you move each finger and sing its number.

      4. Now sing the numbers and play it on the piano keyboard.

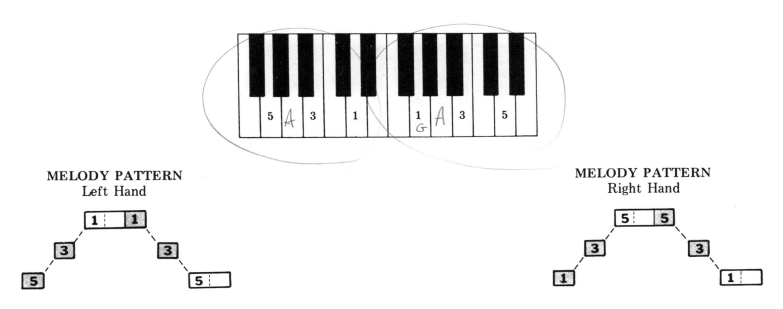

MELODY PATTERN
Left Hand

MELODY PATTERN
Right Hand

Now play "Skips" again using the keys shown here.

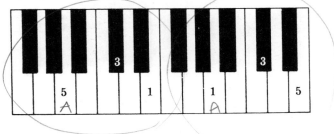

Left Hand

Teacher's Music

Right Hand

2311

SKIPS AND STEPS

Each day do the following as you practice:

1. "Shape" the melody pattern in the air as you sing the finger numbers. Look for the skips, repeated patterns and steps.

   2. Sing the finger numbers — clap the rhythm.

     3. Play this on your arm as you move each finger and sing its number.

      4. Now sing the numbers and play it on the piano keyboard.

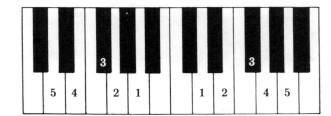

MELODY PATTERN
Left Hand

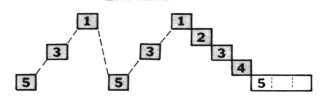

MELODY PATTERN
Right Hand

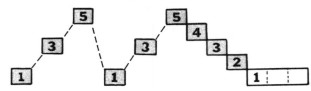

Find these keys and play "Skips and Steps" again.

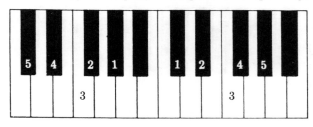

Left Hand

Teacher's Music

Right Hand

SWINGING

ASSIGNED	COMPLETED	COMMENTS:

WEEK	M	T	W	Th	F	S	Su	
1st								
2nd								
3rd								

Do this each day:

1. "Shape" the melody pattern in the air as you sing the finger numbers.
   Here we have steps and one repeated tone.
2. Sing the finger numbers — clap the rhythm.
3. Play this on your arm as you move each finger and sing its number.
4. Now sing the numbers and play it on the piano keyboard.
   Feel the "swing" of the melody.

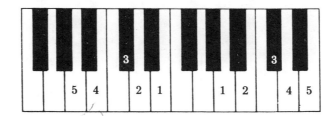

MELODY PATTERN
Left Hand

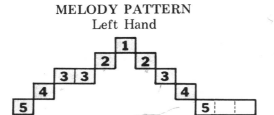

MELODY PATTERN
Right Hand

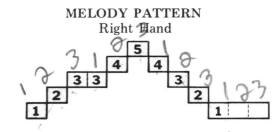

Now play "Swinging" in this new place.

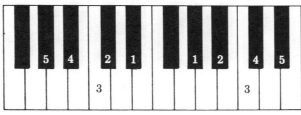

Left Hand

Teacher's Music

Right Hand

OLD WOMAN
(Variation)

Each day:

1. "Shape" the melody pattern in the air as you sing the finger numbers.
   Notice the skips, repeated pattern, repeated notes and steps.

  2. Sing the finger numbers — clap the rhythm.

    3. Play this on your arm as you move each finger and sing its number.

      4. Now sing the numbers and play it on the piano keyboard.

WEEK	M	T	W	Th	F	S	Su	ASSIGNED____ COMPLETED____ COMMENTS:
1st								_____
2nd								_____
3rd								_____

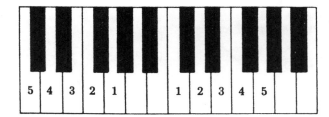

MELODY PATTERN
Left Hand

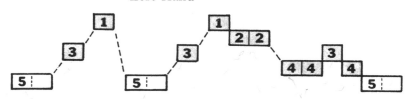

MELODY PATTERN
Right Hand

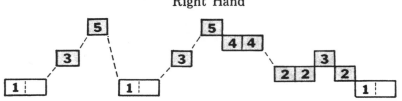

Notice which finger uses the black key as you play "Old Woman" again.

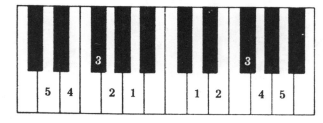

Left Hand

Teacher's Music

Right Hand

2311

OLD MAN
(Variation)

ASSIGNED___ COMPLETED___ COMMENTS:							
WEEK	M	T	W	Th	F	S	Su
1st							
2nd							
3rd							

1. "Shape" the melody pattern in the air as you sing the finger numbers. Notice this melody moves by *steps*.
2. Sing the finger numbers — clap the rhythm.
3. Play this on your arm as you move each finger and sing its number.
4. Now sing the numbers and play it on the piano keyboard.

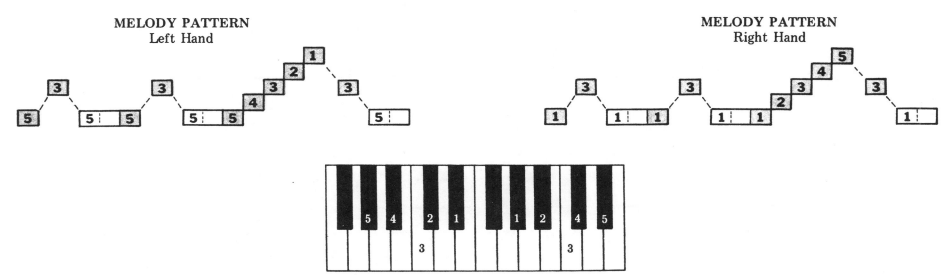

MELODY PATTERN
Left Hand

MELODY PATTERN
Right Hand

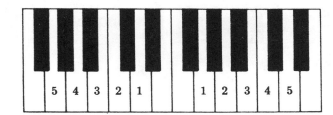

See how many different places you can play all of the songs you have learned so far.
Just remember to play "Up and Down" in each place first so that you will know the right tones to use.

Left Hand

Teacher's Music

Right Hand

8

THE GRAND STAFF

The letter names of the piano keyboard go from A to G.
Play all of the A's, the B's, C's, etc.

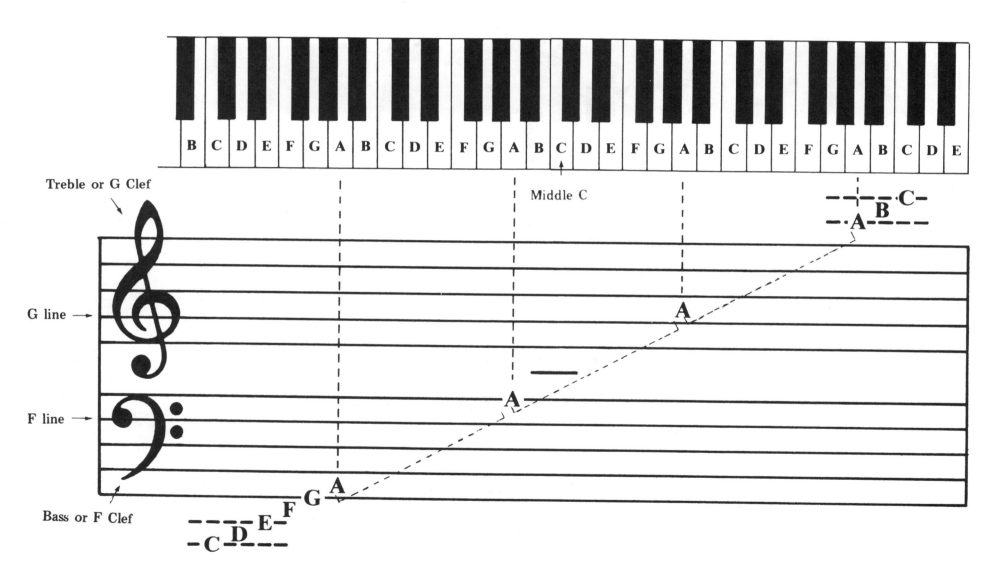

This is the *grand staff*. Fill in the letter names of the lines and spaces. Then each day practice finding each one on your piano.

2311

THE GRAND STAFF

ASSIGNED____ COMPLETED____ COMMENTS:							
WEEK	M	T	W	Th	F	S	Su
1st							
2nd							
3rd							

Write the letter names of the *lines*.

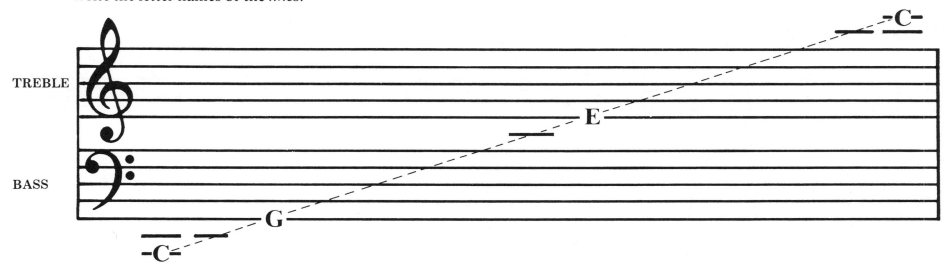

Write the letter names of the *spaces*.

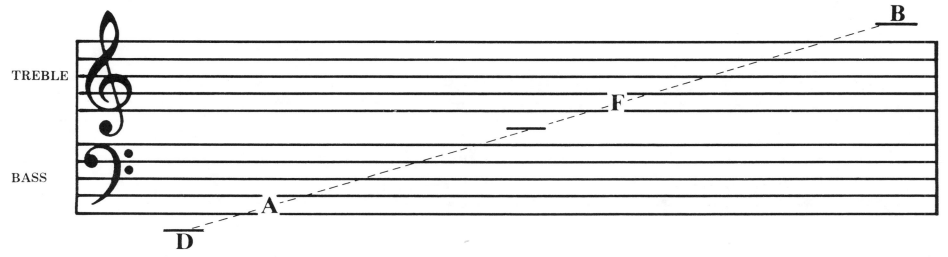

TIME SIGNATURES

First fill in the time signatures for these melodies.
Next play them in the key as written.
Then transpose to other keys.

ASSIGNED___ COMPLETED___	COMMENTS:

WEEK	M	T	W	Th	F	S	Su	
1st								
2nd								
3rd								

Transpose to D♭ and E♭ Major.

Transpose to D and F Major.

Transpose to D♭ and E♭ Major.

KEY SIGNATURES

There are seven flats in
the key of C♭ Major.

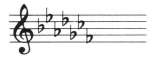

There are seven sharps
in the key of C♯ Major.

But, since there is very little music written in the keys of C♭ or C♯, we shall spend our time on the other six keys.

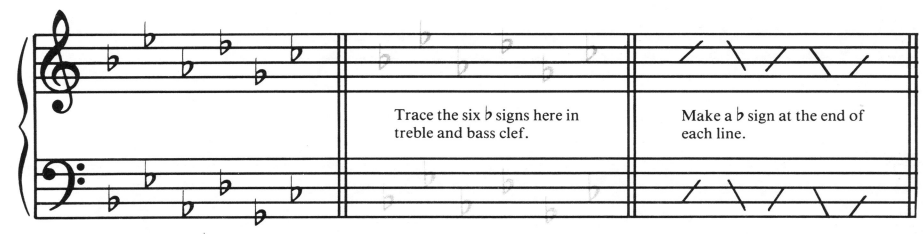

Trace the six ♭ signs here in treble and bass clef.

Make a ♭ sign at the end of each line.

Key of G♭ Major

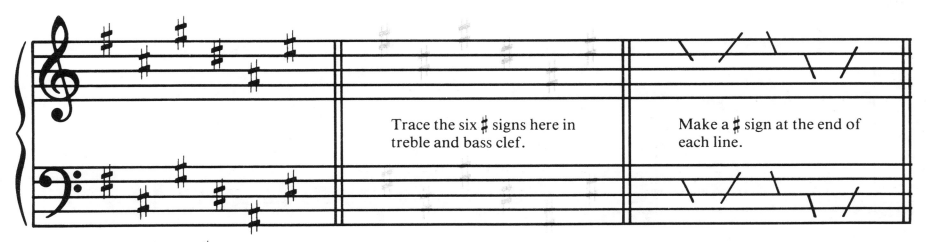

Trace the six ♯ signs here in treble and bass clef.

Make a ♯ sign at the end of each line.

Key of F♯ Major

READING FAMILIAR MELODIES

ASSIGNED___ COMPLETED___ COMMENTS:									
WEEK	M	T	W	Th	F	S	Su		
1st									
2nd									
3rd									

1. Follow the "ups and downs" of this melody as you play first in E♭ then in E and F Major.

2. The rhythm of this piece is the same as "Old Woman," but something has been changed. What is it?
   Play first in F major then transpose to G♭ and G Major.

3. Notice the skips, steps and repeated patterns in this melody.
   Transpose to A♭ and A Major.

ENGLISH FOLK SONG

LINES AND SPACES

ASSIGNED____ COMPLETED____ COMMENTS:							
WEEK	M	T	W	Th	F	S	Su
1st							
2nd							
3rd							

1. Make these notes in both treble and bass clef.

2. Practice making G♭ and F♯ Major key signatures in your *Theory Papers*.
   Then write the G♭ and F♯ Major key signatures as indicated.

PATTERN READING

As you read these melodies look for any patterns such as repeated tones, sequences, or rhythmic patterns. Transpose to different keys each day.

ASSIGNED____ COMPLETED____	COMMENTS:

WEEK	M	T	W	Th	F	S	Su	
1st								
2nd								
3rd								

1.

Transpose to G and E Major.

2.

Transpose to D and F Major.

3.

Transpose to D♭ and D Major.

KEY SIGNATURES

Fill in the missing key signatures.

First practice writing them in your *Theory Papers*.

ASSIGNED____ COMPLETED____	COMMENTS:

WEEK	M	T	W	Th	F	S	Su
1st							
2nd							
3rd							

1.

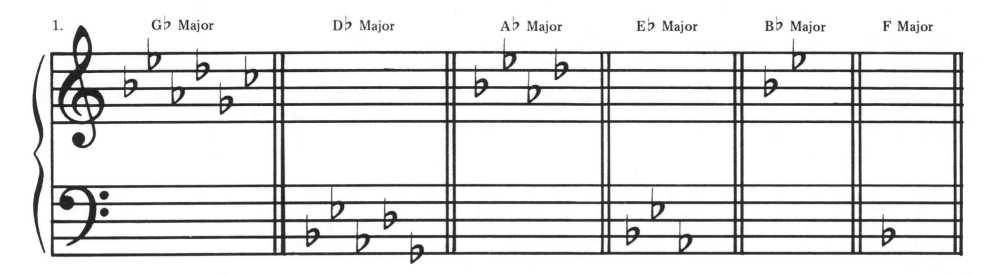

G♭ Major   D♭ Major   A♭ Major   E♭ Major   B♭ Major   F Major

2.

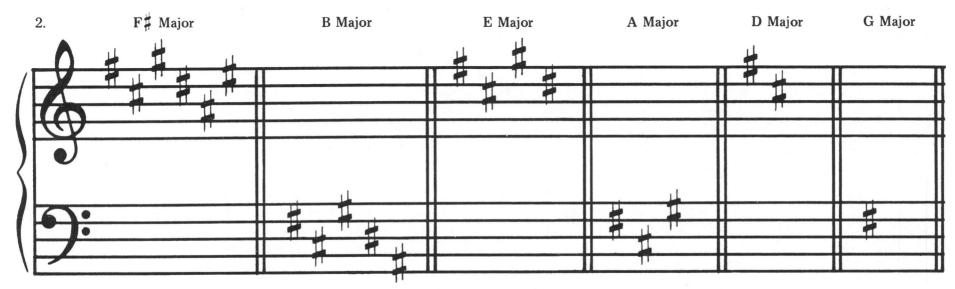

F♯ Major   B Major   E Major   A Major   D Major   G Major

2311

MELODIC MOVEMENT FROM TREBLE TO BASS

ASSIGNED____ COMPLETED____	COMMENTS:

WEEK	M	T	W	Th	F	S	Su	
1st								
2nd								
3rd								

1. How has "Whistle Daughter" been changed here from page 16, *Music for Piano?*
   Transpose to E♭ and F Major.

2. Practice letting your eyes move from 𝄞 to 𝄢 and back to 𝄞 as you play this.

   Keep going! Transpose to D and D♭ Major.

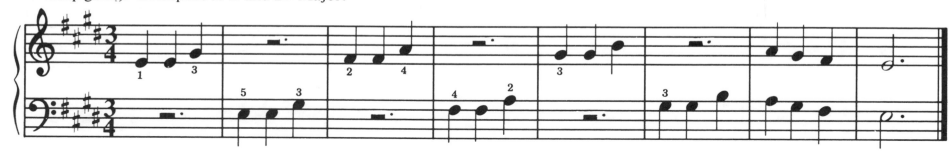

3. Notice where the melody skips from *line to line* and where it moves *space to space*.
   Transpose to A♭ and A Major.

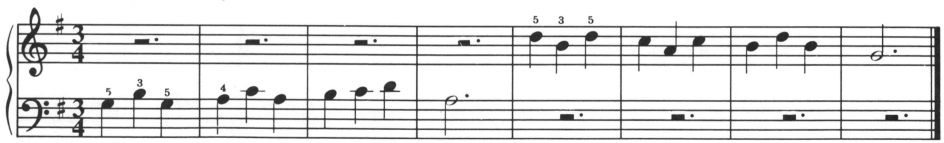

KEY SIGNATURES

Practice making flat and sharp key signatures in your *Theory Papers,* then fill in the key signatures on this page.

1. Make flat key signatures in treble and bass clef.

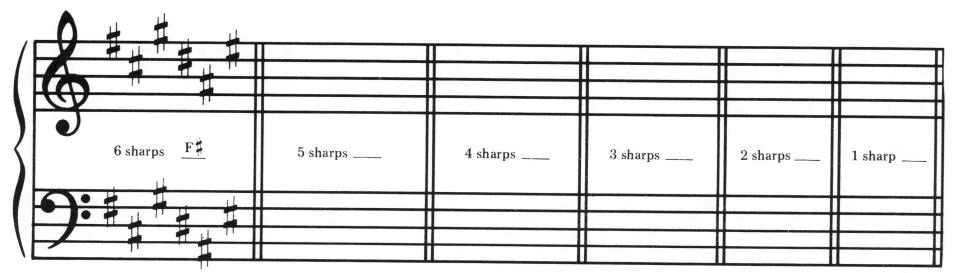

6 flats G♭   5 flats ____   4 flats ____   3 flats ____   2 flats ____   1 flat ____

2. Make sharp key signatures in the treble and bass clefs.

6 sharps F♯   5 sharps ____   4 sharps ____   3 sharps ____   2 sharps ____   1 sharp ____

PLAYING TOGETHER
(Variation)

ASSIGNED____ COMPLETED____								COMMENTS:
WEEK	M	T	W	Th	F	S	Su	_____
1st								_____
2nd								_____
3rd								_____

1. How does this melody differ from "Playing Together" page 18, *Music for Piano?*

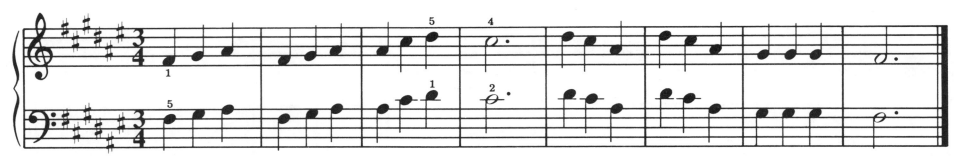

Transpose to F and G Major.

2. To sightread this look for repeated tones, skips, and steps.
Transpose to F and E Major.

THEME AND VARIATION

ASSIGNED____ COMPLETED____								COMMENTS:
WEEK	M	T	W	Th	F	S	Su	
1st								
2nd								
3rd								

1. Here is a theme and variation. First find the theme, then the variation to see where the melody has been changed. Next play the second theme and create your own variation.

2. Each day play this melody and create new variations. At the end of the week, write one on the blank staff.

SEQUENCE

1. Mark all of the sequences in this song.
   Also count the time as you play it.

Transpose to E♭ and D♭ Major.

2. Try to read this as a two-note phrase going from bass to treble or treble to bass.
   Notice the shape of the melody.

Transpose to C, B and B♭ Major.

THEME AND VARIATION

First play the theme to hear it and see the patterns.
Then create variations of your own.
After practicing these and others in *Theory Papers,*
write one for the treble clef and one for the bass clef.

ASSIGNED___ COMPLETED___							COMMENTS:
WEEK	M	T	W	Th	F	S Su	
1st							
2nd							
3rd							

1.   Theme

Your Variation

2.   Theme

Your Variation

MELODIC VARIATION

1. Before sightreading this variation of ''Casey Jones,''
   find all the patterns that are repeated.
   Don't look at your hands as you play it.
   Transpose to A♭ and A Major.

EXPRESSION IN SIGHTREADING

2. When sightreading, don't forget the expression.
   Transpose to D♭ and E♭ Major.

QUESTION AND ANSWER

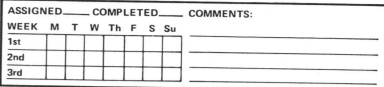

1. This question has two different answers.
   Use the same question to create new answers.

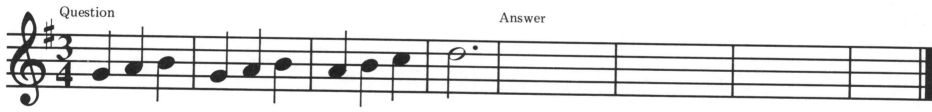

2. Create five new answers to these questions each day and at the end of the week, write down one answer.

IMITATION

1. The right hand imitates the left hand in this "follow the leader" type of song.
   Figure out all of the patterns before you play it.
   Each day transpose up or down to different keys.

MELODIC LINES

2. Both parts of this song move in the same direction (parallel motion).
   Notice where it moves by steps, by skips, or where it stays the same.

Each day transpose to one of these keys: D, D♭, C, E, F, F♯ Major.

QUESTION AND ANSWER

Use the rhythm of the question in your answer but create many different melody lines.

Create at least three answers for each question before going on to the next one.

Also practice the questions and answers in *Theory Papers*.

1.

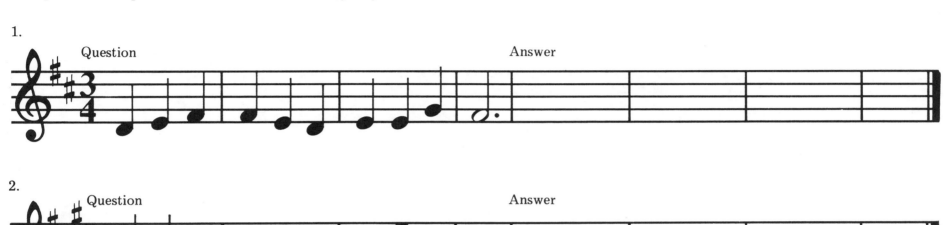

2.

3.

4.

READING STACCATO NOTES

ASSIGNED____ COMPLETED____ COMMENTS:								
WEEK	M	T	W	Th	F	S	Su	
1st								
2nd								
3rd								

1. Even though it may be difficult to play this melody staccato,
   do not look at your hands as you play it.

Transpose to B and D Major.

2. Look for the skips, steps, and repeated patterns in this melody as you play it slowly.
   Also be sure to observe the dynamics.

Transpose to E♭ and G♭ Major.

3. Be sure to make a separate stroke for each staccato note.
   Also make the staccato eighth notes shorter than the quarter notes.

Transpose to D and F Major.

MAJOR TRIAD SETS

ASSIGNED____ COMPLETED____ COMMENTS:								
WEEK	M	T	W	Th	F	S	Su	
1st								
2nd								
3rd								

1. Make the three triads that are all white in treble and bass clef.

Make the three triads with the black key in the middle.

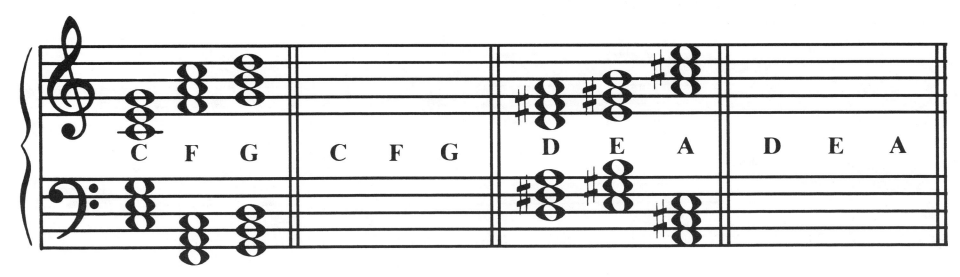

2. Write the following triads in treble and bass clef.

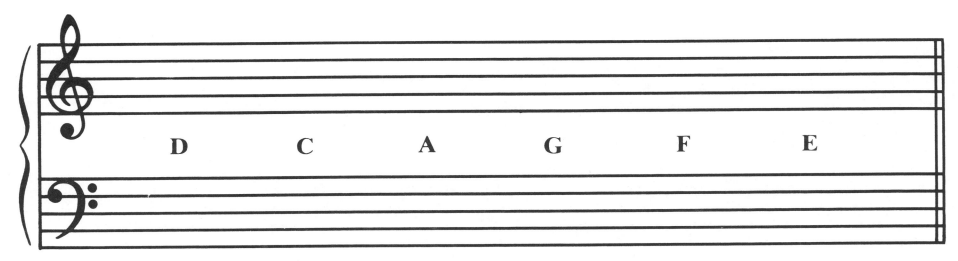

2311

THE I CHORD

ASSIGNED____ COMPLETED____ COMMENTS:									
WEEK	M	T	W	Th	F	S	Su		
1st									
2nd									
3rd									

1. As you play this melody each day practice shaping the melody at the same time you recognize the chords in the left hand. Transpose to E and E♭ Major.

2. Notice that in the first phrase the melody is in the left hand with the chords in the right. And in the second phrase the melody is in the right hand with the harmony played with the left hand. "Count" the rhythm before you try to play it. Transpose to C and E Major.

MAJOR TRIAD SETS

ASSIGNED____ COMPLETED____								COMMENTS:
WEEK	M	T	W	Th	F	S	Su	
1st								
2nd								
3rd								

1. Write each chord as indicated then play them on the piano.

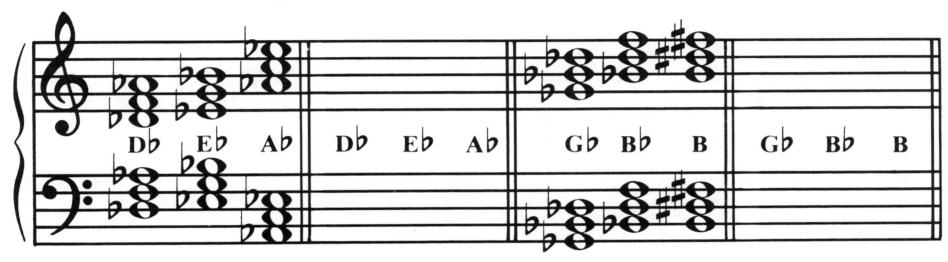

CHORD SONG

2. Improvise chord songs over the F Major triad then write one using the rhythm of these first two bars.

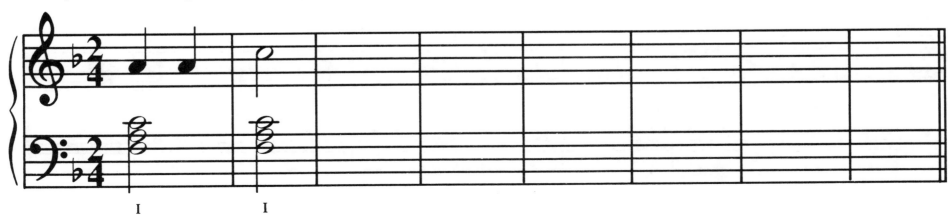

CHORD TONES

ASSIGNED_____				COMPLETED_____			COMMENTS:	
WEEK	M	T	W	Th	F	S	Su	
1st								
2nd								
3rd								

1. This melody is composed of tones from the I and V₇ chords.
   Transpose to B and B♭ Major.

PASSING TONES

2. Watch carefully to see the shape of the melody and chord changes.
   Also be prepared when the melody moves from the treble to bass clef.
   Play as written, then transpose to E and G Major.

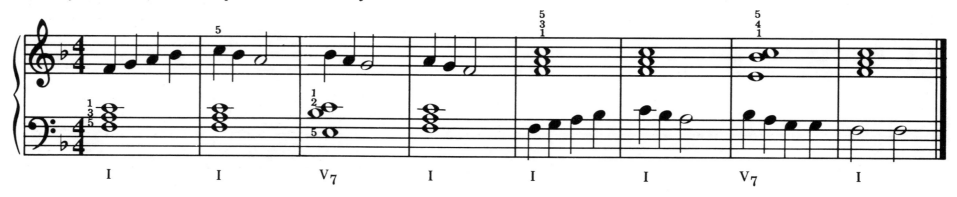

I V₇ I

Each day play the I V₇ I chords in the keys shown here.
Also, each day, write the missing chords for one of the keys.
Play these very smoothly with nicely curved fingers.

ASSIGNED____ COMPLETED____ COMMENTS:								
WEEK	M	T	W	Th	F	S	Su	
1st								
2nd								
3rd								

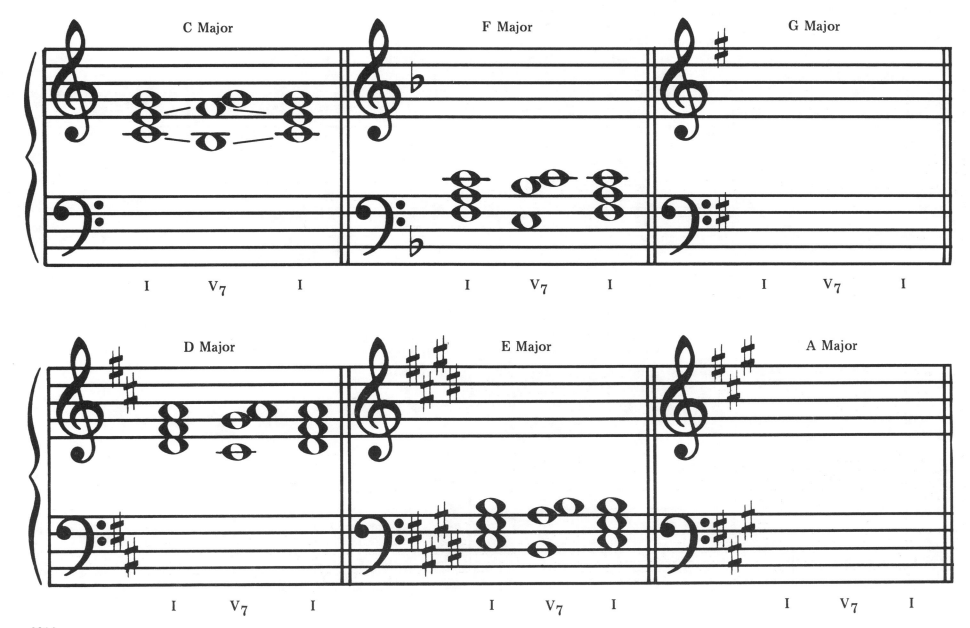

PARALLEL AND CONTRARY MOTION

ASSIGNED			COMPLETED				COMMENTS:
WEEK	M	T	W	Th	F	S	Su
1st							
2nd							
3rd							

1. First play the melody in the right hand as you play "block" chords in the left hand.
   Next look through the entire song to see the shape of the lines in both the treble and bass clefs.
   Notice where they move in parallel motion and where they move in contrary motion.
   It might be helpful to mark in the direction as indicated by the lines in the first two measures.
   Transpose to D♭ and E♭ Major.

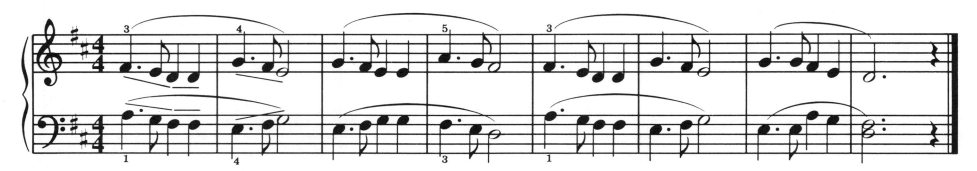

STACCATO MELODY

2. Notice the similarities and differences in this melody and "Tip Toes" in *Music for Piano*.
   Some things have been changed while other things have remained the same.
   Which of these three have been changed: melody, harmony, or rhythm?
   Transpose to B and D♭ Major.

2311

QUESTIONS AND ANSWERS

1. This question is harmonized by incomplete chords in the left hand.
   Make up three answers each day using the same bass style.
   Finally, make up new questions of your own in other keys.

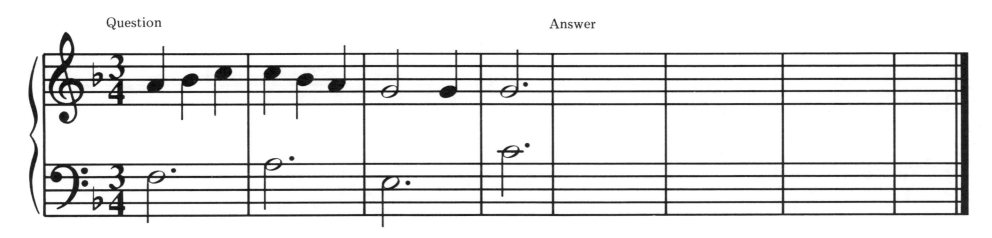

2. This question is in the left hand, the harmony is in the right.
   Make up both parallel and contrasting answers in the left hand with chords in the right hand.
   You may also want to try another chord pattern.

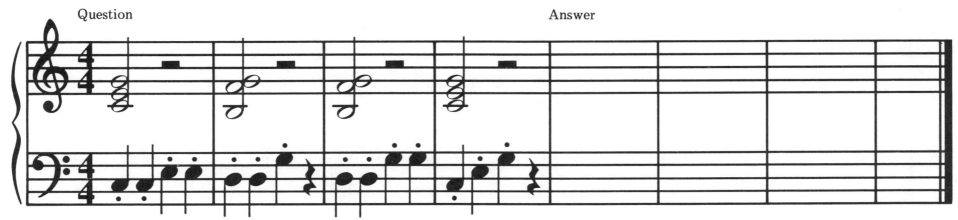

LOOBY LOO
(Variation)

ASSIGNED____ COMPLETED____ COMMENTS:								
WEEK	M	T	W	Th	F	S	Su	
1st								
2nd								
3rd								

1. First look through this to find all of the melodic, harmonic and rhythmic patterns.
   Then play it slowly with two strong beats or pulses in each measure.
   Be sure to keep going.

Transpose to Db and Eb Major.

NOTE PATTERNS

2. Notice where this melody has repeated tones and where it moves by skips.

Transpose to F and D Major.

QUESTIONS AND ANSWERS

ASSIGNED___ COMPLETED___	COMMENTS:							
WEEK	M	T	W	Th	F	S	Su	
1st								
2nd								
3rd								

1. Play this question with a feeling of two pulses or beats in each measure.
   Create at least two parallel and two contrasting answers each day.

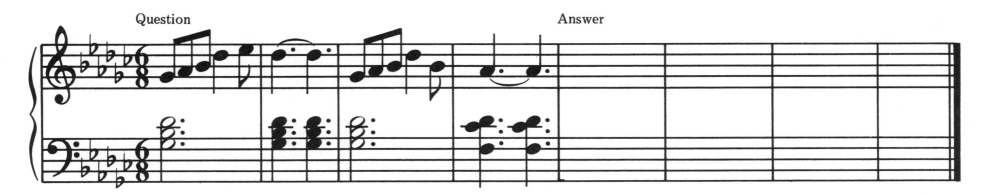

2. Create answers which have repetitions, sequences and inversions.
   Harmonize your questions and answers with either block chords or single note patterns.

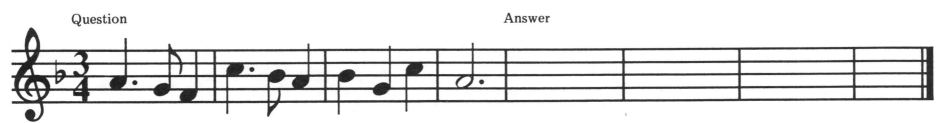

3. Write the following key signatures.　　　　Write the following chords in treble and bass clef.

WALTZ BASS

1. In playing a waltz, be sure that the second and third beats of the accompaniment are lighter than the first beat.

Transpose to D and Db Major.

2. Play the left hand chords with a "down-up" motion of the wrist.

Transpose to B and Bb Major.

MELODIC PATTERNS

3. Notice the various repeated note patterns. Find the sequences.

Transpose to Eb and Db Major.

MELODY STUDY

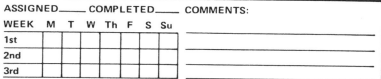

WEEK	M	T	W	Th	F	S	Su	COMMENTS:
1st								
2nd								
3rd								

1. Write the I and V₇ chords for this melody, then create many different answers with these chords.

2. First write the I and V₇ chords in the bass clef. Then create different melodies each day for these chords. Notate one of your melodies.

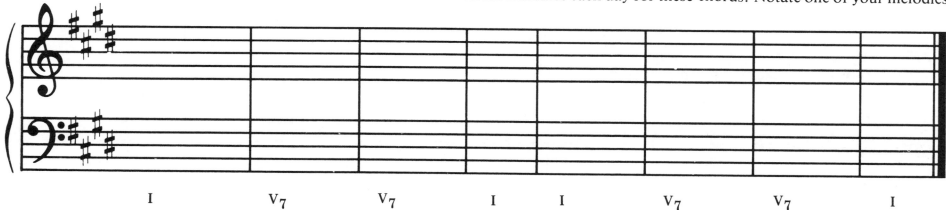

3. Improvise different melodies for this waltz bass each day.   Then notate one and be sure to put in dynamics.

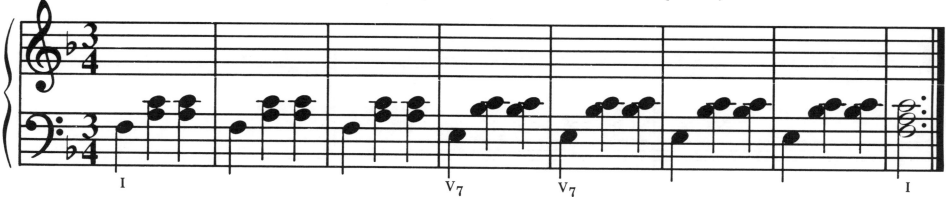

ASSIGNED____ COMPLETED____	COMMENTS:
WEEK M T W Th F S Su	
1st	
2nd	
3rd	

1. Play the second and third beats in the left hand much softer than the first.

Transpose to G and A♭ Major.

EXTENDED PATTERNS

2. These melodies use six notes of the scale.
   Do not look at your hands as you practice these.

Transpose to D♭ and C Major.

Transpose to G and A♭ Major.

2311

QUESTIONS AND ANSWERS

ASSIGNED____ COMPLETED____	COMMENTS:
WEEK M T W Th F S Su	_____
1st	_____
2nd	_____
3rd	_____

1. Create two parallel and two contrasting answers each day for these questions.

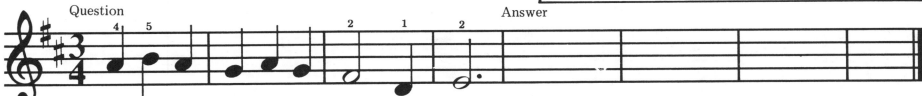

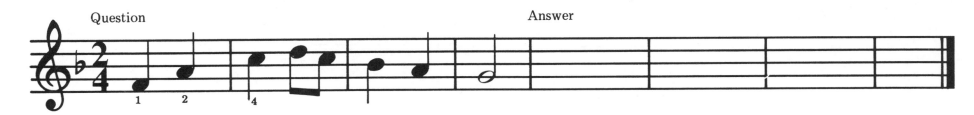

2. Create contrasting answers for this pentatonic question.

3. Fill in the following major triads.

C   F   G   D   E   A   Db   Eb   Ab   Gb   Bb   B

2311

MINOR MELODIES

1. Look for all similarities and differences in this melody.

NORWEGIAN FOLK SONG

Transpose to e and c minor.

2. Look for the rhythmic, melodic and harmonic patterns in this piece.

Transpose to d, f and g minor.

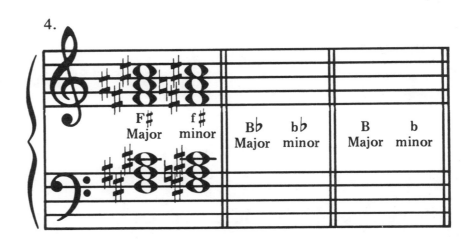

MINOR TRIADS

Remember that a major chord (triad) becomes minor when the middle note is lowered one half step, (the next closest tone).

<table>
<tr><td>ASSIGNED_____ COMPLETED_____ COMMENTS:</td></tr>
</table>

WEEK	M	T	W	Th	F	S	Su		
1st									
2nd									
3rd									

1. Write each chord first in major then in minor.

| C Major | c minor | F Major | f minor | G Major | g minor |

2.

| D Major | d minor | E Major | e minor | A Major | a minor |

3.

| Dᵇ Major | *dᵇ minor | Eᵇ Major | eᵇ minor | Aᵇ Major | aᵇ minor |

4.

| F♯ Major | f♯ minor | Bᵇ Major | bᵇ minor | B Major | b minor |

*usually written as c♯ minor.

Practice with your key signature and major and minor chord flash cards.

2311

MINOR MELODY

ASSIGNED___ COMPLETED___ COMMENTS:

WEEK	M	T	W	Th	F	S	Su	
1st								
2nd								
3rd								

1. Find the similarities between this melody and "Surprises," page 42, *Music for Piano*.

Transpose to d, e♭ and f minor.

DORIAN SONG

2. This song uses the Dorian mode.
   Notice how the melody changes every two measures, yet the left hand bass part stays the same.

MINOR MELODY

ASSIGNED____ COMPLETED____ COMMENTS:								
WEEK	M	T	W	Th	F	S	Su	_____
1st								_____
2nd								_____
3rd								_____

1. Play the I and V_7 chords as written here then transpose up by half steps to all keys.

I V_7 I

2. Write a melody for these chords in d minor.

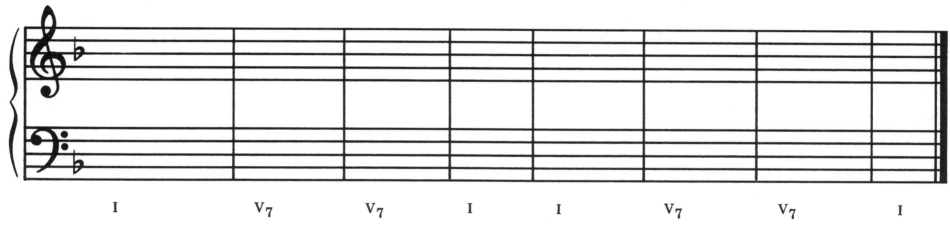

I V_7 V_7 I   I V_7 V_7 I

QUESTION AND ANSWER

3. Create answers for this question using the I and V_7 chords.

I   I   I V_7

PATTERN READING

ASSIGNED____ COMPLETED____ COMMENTS:								
WEEK	M	T	W	Th	F	S	Su	____
1st								____
2nd								____
3rd								____

1. Play the left hand part very softly as you let the right hand melody sing out.

Transpose to B and D Major.

2. Look for rhythmic patterns in the second phrase which are similar to those in the first.

Transpose to E♭ and F♯ Major.

QUESTION AND ANSWER

ASSIGNED____ COMPLETED____ COMMENTS:								
WEEK	M	T	W	Th	F	S	Su	____
1st								____
2nd								____
3rd								____

1. Each day create both parallel and contrasting answers for this question.

2. Make up answers to this question using the Pentatonic scale.

3. Write the following triads:

4. Write these key signatures.

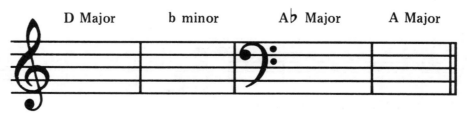

2311

REVIEW

| ASSIGNED_____ COMPLETED_____ COMMENTS: |
WEEK	M	T	W	Th	F	S	Su
1st							
2nd							
3rd							

1. Which measures in each phrase are alike
   and which are different?

Transpose to C and E Major.

2. Notice the rhythmic and melodic patterns.

Transpose to c and e minor.

3. Where do the parts move in the same direction and where do they go in opposite directions?

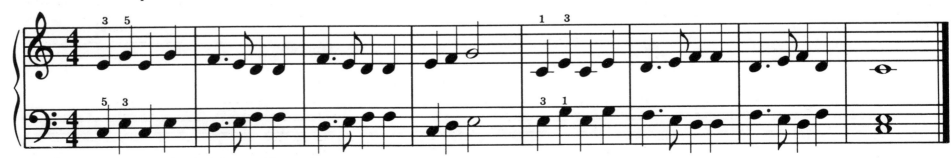

Transpose to B and D♭ Major.

TRIAD STUDY

ASSIGNED_____ COMPLETED_____	COMMENTS:							
WEEK	M	T	W	Th	F	S	Su	_____
1st								_____
2nd								_____
3rd								_____

1. Create both parallel and contrasting answers to this question.

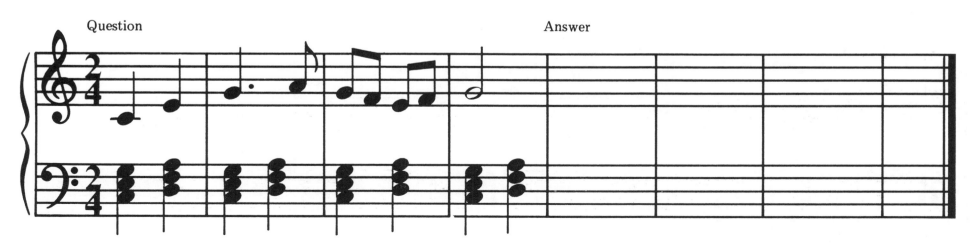

QUESTION AND ANSWER

2. Make up new answers each day to this question.

KEY SIGNATURE REVIEW

ASSIGNED____ COMPLETED____ COMMENTS:							
WEEK	M	T	W	Th	F	S	Su
1st							
2nd							
3rd							

1. Make these major key signatures in treble and bass clef and name each key.

2. Make these minor key signatures in treble and bass clef and name each key.

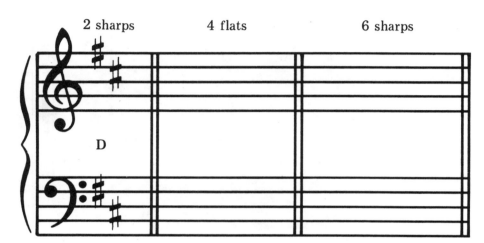

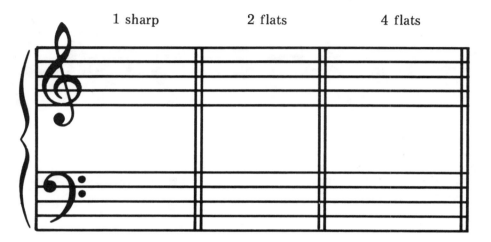

CHORD REVIEW

3. Write the following major triads.

4. Write the following minor triads.

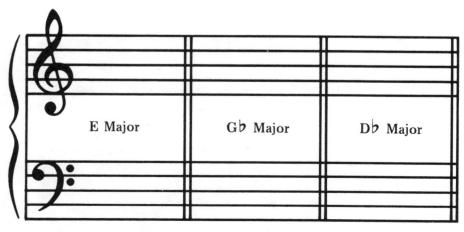